Dicey's Song

A Novel Study

By Jane Kotinek

Copyright © 2012 by Jane Kotinek. All rights reserved.

ISBN -13:978-1478296997
ISBN-10:1478296992

The classroom teacher may reproduce copies of materials in this book for classroom use only. The reproduction of any part for an entire school or school system is strictly prohibited. No part of this publication may be transmitted, stored, or recorded in any form without permission from the author.

Table of Contents

Page	Content
3	Vocabulary List for entire book
4	Description
5- 9	Vocabulary Words Activities and Worksheets
10- 17	Chapters 1- 5 Questions with Essay Prompts
18-19	Venn diagram with Essay
20- 28	Chapters 6- 12 Questions and Essay Prompt
29	Character Trait Chart with Textual Proof
30	Internal/External Conflicts Activity
31	Cause and Effect Chart Activity
32	Analyzing Title Activity
33	Analyzing Theme Activity
34	Character Analysis Activity
35-36	Plot Diagram with Plot Summarization Activity
37- 50	Teacher's Edition
38- 42	Vocabulary Worksheet Answers
43- 50	Answers to Chapter Questions
51-69	Assessments
52- 54	Quiz 1 Chapters 1 - 3
55- 56	Quiz 2 Chapters 4- 6
57- 58	Quiz 3 Chapters 7-8
59- 60	Quiz 4 Chapters 9- 12
61- 68	Comprehension Test
69	Answers to Quizzes and Test

Dicey's Song A Novel Study

This novel study is to be used in the classroom with the novel <u>Dicey's Song</u> by Cynthia Voight.

This 70-page novel study includes: open-ended questions for the entire book, vocabulary list, quizzes, comprehension test, and language arts activities. The activities include: vocabulary worksheets, dictionary practice, and crossword puzzle, theme analysis, cause and effect activity, internal/external conflict chart activity, character traits with textual proof activity, essay prompts, plot diagram with summarization essay, character analysis essay, and a Venn diagram with essay.

Answer keys are included for the questions, vocabulary worksheets, quizzes, and comprehension test.

Vocabulary List

1. chastened (52)
2. exhilarating (92)
3. envied (107)
4. sag (116)
5. appreciated (131)
6. extremes (138)
7. quivered (161)
8. curious (169)
9. eagerly (187)
10. exclusion (191)
11. impassive (200)
12. impatiently (205)
13. wisdom (218)
14. contentment (241)
15. emerged (248)
16. impressed (263)
17. charisma (280)
18. scurried (294)
19. reverberated (295)
20. solemn (327)

Directions: Put the words in alphabetical order on the lines below. Start from the beginning of the alphabet.

1. _____
2. _____
3. _____
4. _____
5. _____
6. _____
7. _____
8. _____
9. _____
10. _____

11. _____
12. _____
13. _____
14. _____
15. _____
16. _____
17. _____
18. _____
19. _____
20. _____

Vocabulary List with Definitions

appreciated	To be aware of value or significance
charisma	A personal quality that produce feelings of devotion or enthusiasm
chastened	To reprimand or punish
contentment	The state of being satisfied, happy
curious	Questioning or prying
eagerly	Showing an interest in, enthusiastic about
emerged	To come forth, to be revealed
envied	Felt resentment or jealously toward someone
exclusion	Keep out, reject
exhilarating	Stimulating, energizing, elating
extremes	Very intense, remote, to the greatest degree
impassive	Expressionless, showing no emotion
impatiently	Restlessly, anxiously
impressed	To affect favorably, to have left a mark
quivered	To shake or vibrate
reverberated	To echo continuously
sag	To droop, to lose firmness
scurried	To scamper or skitter about
solemn	Gloomy, somber
wisdom	Common sense, good judgment, knowing what is right

Vocabulary Activity #1

appreciated	eagerly	extremes	reverberated
charisma	emerged	impassive	sag
chastened	envied	impatiently	scurried
contentment	exclusion	impressed	solemn
curious	exhilarating	quivered	wisdom

Directions: Unscramble the vocabulary word and write it on the space provided.

1. gas _____
2. patimeitnyl _____
3. dvneei _____
4. dswmoi _____
5. pmssaieiv _____
6. aaieeppcrtd _____
7. degreme _____
8. eetttnocneenm _____
9. srcuuoi _____
10. brrrvdteeeea _____
11. eeemrtxs _____
12. caimasih _____
13. rrieudcs _____
14. dssrpmeei _____
15. eeaylgr _____
16. lhixeeaigntr _____
17. mneols _____
18. drvuqiee _____
19. xlsncuioe _____
20. denetsahc _____

Vocabulary Activity #1

appreciated	eagerly	extremes	reverberated
charisma	emerged	impassive	sag
chastened	envied	impatiently	scurried
contentment	exclusion	impressed	solemn
curious	exhilarating	quivered	wisdom

Directions: Find the missing vowels for each vocabulary word and write the vocabulary word on the space provided.

1. c__r__ __ __s _____
2. r__v__rb__r__t__d _____
3. __xtr__m__s _____
4. ch__r__sm__ _____
5. sc__rr__ __d _____
6. __mpr__ss__d _____
7. s__g _____
8. __mp__t__ __ntl__ _____
9. __nv__ __d _____
10. w__sd__m _____
11. __ppr__c__ __t__d _____
12. __mp__ss__v__ _____
13. c__nt__ntm__nt _____
14. __m__rg__d _____
15. ch__st__n__d _____
16. __xcl__s__ __n _____
17. q__ __v__r__d _____
18. __xh__l__r__t__ng _____
19. s__l__mn _____
20. __ __g__rl__ _____

© 2012 Jane Kotinek   Dicey's Song A Novel Study

Vocabulary Activity #3

Directions: Use the dictionary guide words to decide whether the vocabulary word falls before the first guide word, between the guide words, or after the guide words. Place an X in the correct box.

Vocabulary Word	Guide Words	Before Guide Words	Between Guide Words	After Guide Words
appreciated	apothegm/applicator			
charisma	chariot/ chaste			
chastened	charge/ chase			
contentment	context/ continue			
curious	curate/curse			
eagerly	early/easel			
emerged	egg/eject			
envied	entertain/envoy			
exclusion	excoriate/exhale			
exhilarating	exhaust/exhort			
extremes	explosion/ extend			
impassive	impair/imperious			
impatiently	impede/ import			
impressed	impost/improvise			
quivered	quintet/quoth			
reverberated	retch/return			
sag	sage/saint			
scurried	scurvy/seal			
solemn	soda/solace			
wisdom	wire/with			

Vocabulary Crossword Puzzle

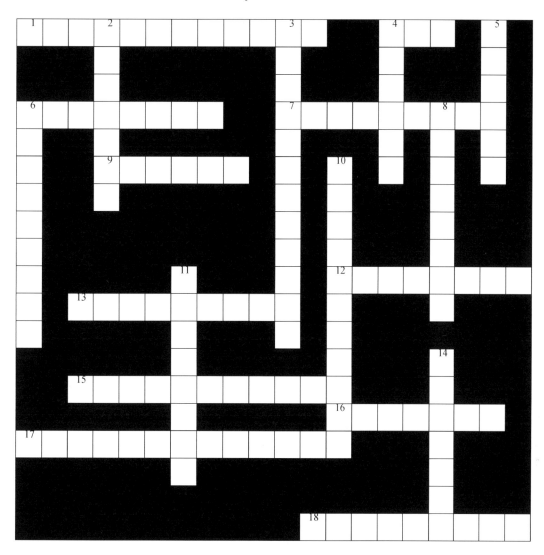

Across
1. To echo continuously
4. To droop, to lose firmness
6. A personal quality that produce feelings of devotion or enthusiasm
7. To affect favorably, to have left a mark
9. Felt resentment or jealously toward someone
12. Very intense, remote, to the greatest degree
13. Keep out, reject
15. The state of being satisfied, happy
16. Showing an interest in, enthusiastic about
17. Restlessly, anxiously
18. Expressionless, showing no emotion

Down
2. To come forth, to be revealed
3. Stimulating, energizing, elating
4. Gloomy, somber
5. Good judgment, knowing what is right
6. To reprimand or punish
8. To scamper or skitter about
10. To be aware of value or significance
11. To shake or vibrate
14. Questioning or prying

© 2012 Jane Kotinek   Dicey's Song A Novel Study

Dicey's Song A Novel Study

Chapter 1 pages 1-37

1. Where did Dicey and her family go to live?

2. What happened to Dicey's boat?

3. Why did Dicey want to fix the sailboat?

4. What was the purpose of Dicey getting a job?

5. What is wrong with Maybeth?

6. Why did Dicey go to Millie Tydings for a job?

7. What reasons did Dicey give for why Millie should hire her?

8. How much money would Dicey earn per week at the grocery story?

9. What did Gram say families always did first?

10. Why does Gram have an appointment downtown?

11. Where is Dicey's mom?

12. Why is Dicey's mother there?

13. What did James point to in the Bible?

14. What did Gram add to the Bible?

15. Why does James wonder how things will be for them?

16. How does Dicey show that she is maturing?

17. What did Gram ask Dicey to help her with on Sunday?

18. What was on the table waiting for Dicey when she got home from school?

19. Who was the letter from?

20. Why was Dicey upset when she saw who had written the letter?

Chapter 2 Pages 38 – 66

1. What was the name of the girl in class who came up with interesting answers?

2. What was conflict was brought up in class by Wilhemina?

3. Who did Dicey see at the bike rack?

4. What was the boy doing?

5. *"Is it an hour already?" Millie asked. She turned over a fat wrist to look at her watch. "I'm being awful slow with this."*
   "You had interruptions," Dicey reminded her.

   "That's right," Millie sounded surprised. She couldn't have forgotten, Dicey knew.

   What, if anything, is the above quote foreshadowing?

6. Why is Dicey upset that Sammy interrupted her while she was working on the boat?

7. Why wouldn't Dicey let Sammy help her?

8. Why did Mr. Lingerle want Maybeth to take special lessons?

9. What was Dicey's idea to pay for Maybeth's lessons?

10. What did most of the people think about Gram?

11. Who asked Dicey to be her science partner?

12. What did Gram have for Dicey when she came home from school?

13. What did James hope to do for a job?

14. What announcement did Sammy make in regards to helping James at his job?

15. Why does Dicey feel as though everyone is turning away from her?

Chapter 3 Pages 67 – 102
1. What information did the letter concerning Dicey's mother contain?

2. Why do you think Dicey keeps asking Gram what the letter says?

3. What was Dicey pleased about that Sammy wasn't doing at school?

4. What differences did Dicey see happening with

    Maybeth:

    Sammy:

    James:

5. What was the name of the person playing the guitar?

6. Why did Millie end up with so many boxes of corn flakes?

7. What solution did Dicey come up with to get rid of them?

8. What reason did Millie give for not ordering correctly?

9. What did Millie tell Dicey about the job at the grocery store?

10. Compared to her homework how did Maybeth perform on the piano?

11. What did Gram make a dress out of for Maybeth?

12. What does this tell us about Gram's character?

13. What did Cousin Eunice think of the Tillerman's?

14. Why did Cousin Eunice take the kids in?

15. Why did Mina accuse Dicey of being hard to befriend?

16. Who was the person at the piano waiting to speak to Gram?

17. Why did he have to wait to ask Gran a question?

18. While at dinner, what did Mr. Lingerle do that surprised Dicey?

19. What question did Mr. Lingerle ask Gram to convince her to let Maybeth have piano lessons?

20. What was Mr. Lingerle going to charge for teaching Maybeth?

21. Why were the girls laughing at Dicey in Home EC class?

Essay Question: If Dicey were going to school with you, do you think you could be friends with her? Explain your answer.

Chapter 4 Pages 103 – 136

1. Why didn't Dicey want Sammy to bother her while she worked on the boat?

2. Why did Gram get upset with the kids for going up into the attic?

3. Why do you think Gram doesn't talk about her children?

4. Who did Gram ask to watch the kids so she and Dicey could have a day out on Saturday?

5. Why didn't Gram like to be helped?

6. Why did Dicey enjoy the shopping trip?

7. What was Gram planning to do with the wool?

8. What is the progress of Maybeth's education?

9. Why did Gram say Dicey deserved to enjoy their lunch at the restaurant without having to worry about the price?

10. How long would Dicey have to worry about her brothers and sister?

11. Why did James write a different report?

12. What does James like to work?

13. Why did Gram want to get Dicey a jumper for school?

14. What did the saleslady say about Dicey?

15. Why does Dicey want to ask James about Maybeth?

Essay Question: The shopping trip taken by Dicey and Gram probably changed their relationship. How do you think their relationship changed? Do you think it will be a good or bad change?

_____
_____
_____
_____
_____
_____
_____
_____
_____
_____
_____
_____
_____

Chapter 5 Pages 136-169

1. Why did Dicey regret building a fire?

2. Why did Gram tell Mr. Lingerle he might as well stay while they discussed Maybeth?

3. Why was Gram disappointed with James' ideas about Maybeth?

4. What does James think is the problem with Maybeth?

5. What is his suggestion for Maybeth?

6. Why did Dicey feel the hopelessness surrounding Maybeth was fading away?

7. What is Gram teaching Maybeth to do?

8. What kind of relationship, outside of brother/sister, do Dicey and Sammy appear to have?

9. Why does Sammy get upset with Dicey when he visits her by the boat?

10. Why was Sammy excited when Dicey asked him to get the sandpaper?

11. Why doesn't Sammy play games during recess at school?

12. Why does Sammy think it's his fault about his mother leaving?

13. What was Sammy trying to convince Gram to buy?

14. Whose house would James visit for the first time?

15. Explain why this was considered a big deal for James?

16. Why hasn't James come up with a solution for Maybeth?

17. Why was Maybeth upset when she returned from school?

18. What did James tell Maybeth he was going to do for her?

19. What did James want to use to teach Maybeth?

20. What was his reasoning for his decision?

Essay Question: How do you think Sammy felt about being responsible for his mother leaving the family? How would this feeling of guilt effect him and his behavior? Have you ever felt guilty about doing something that you later regretted? What did you do to correct the situation?

Compare/Contrast Activity

Directions: Compare and contrast (show the similarities and differences) between Dicey and Mina. Use at least 3 examples for each. Be sure to label each circle with the proper heading.

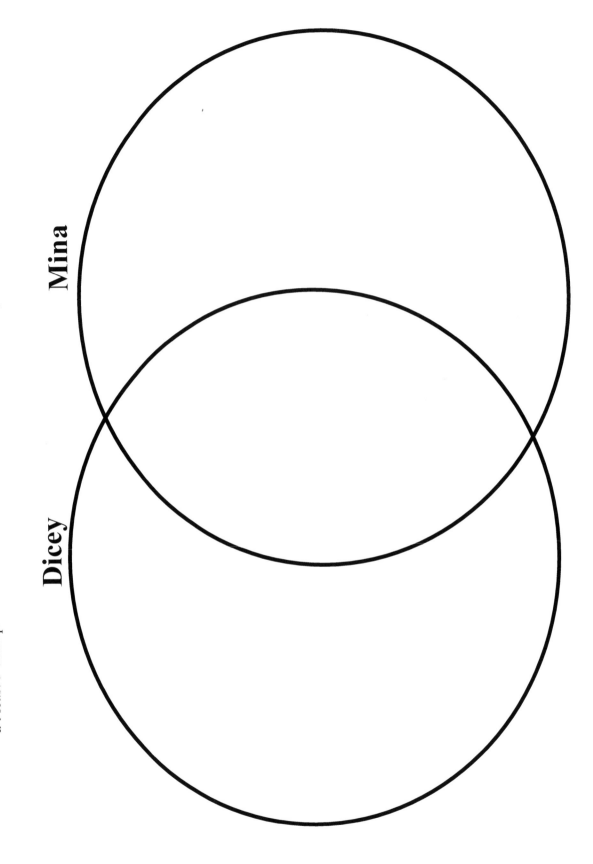

© 2012 Jane Kotinek — <u>Dicey's Song</u> A Novel Study

Compare/Contrast Activity

Directions: Using the Venn Diagram above, write an essay comparing and contrasting Dicey and Mina. Be sure you do not create a list in your essay. Use signal words for compare/contrast (First, for instance, compared to, etc.) to write your essay.

Chapter 6 Pages 170-192

1. What grade did Dicey receive in Home Ec?

2. Why was Dicey upset about the grade?

3. Why was Dicey confused about the grade she received in English?

4. Why did Dicey feel like hugging Gram after they had discussed her report card?

5. Who came into Millie's store while Dicey was working?

6. What did Millie say Gram was like in school?

7. Why did Dicey need to wait for Sammy?

8. Why did Sammy kiss Margaret?

9. What did Maybeth tell Dicey about learning to read?

10. Why did Dicey have an easy time planning a budget with $50?

11. What did Miss Eversleigh do to Dicey's paper with the meals on it?

12. Why didn't Dicey care what Miss Eversleigh thought or said?

Essay Question: Why do you think Dicey shows little concern about the grades she receives in Home Ec? What does this tell us about her character?

Chapter 7 Pages 193- 22

1. Explain Dicey's thoughts on grades and the importance of assignments.

2. What had happened to Dicey's mom?

3. What compliment did Mina give to Dicey?

4. What was Mr. Chappelle accusing Dicey of doing with her story?

5. How did Dicey react to Mr. Chappelle's accusation?

6. What did Mina say about Dicey to defend her to Mr. Chappelle?

7. How did Mina prove Dicey had written the essay?

8. What did Mr. Chappelle do when Dicey picked up her essay?

9. Why do you think Gram forced Dicey to discuss the English paper?

10. What did Gram tell Dicey after she had read Dicey's essay?

11. What did Gram say about her marriage to John?

12. According to Gram, what was the purpose of the essay?

13. Why did Mina's dad reprimand Dicey when she called?

14. Why did Dicey call Mina?

15. Why would Gram worry about what Mina's parents think about her?

Essay Question: Think about Dicey's opinions about grades. Do you think this is a true reflection of grades? What do you think would happen if grades were not given to students? How would teachers know whether a student understood what had been taught?

Chapter 8 Pages 223-266

1. Why didn't Millie ask Dicey for her work paper?

2. Why do you think Dicey didn't mind Mina asking if the essay were about Dicey's momma?

3. Why was Sammy at the grocery store when Dicey got there?

4. Why won't Sammy tell Dicey about the fight he was involved in?

5. Why did James act like he didn't care who Sammy had fought?

6. Why doesn't Maybeth like Ernie?

7. What bargain did Gram try to make with Sammy in connection with the marbles?

8. Describe Sammy.

9. How does Dicey see Jeff?

10. How would you describe Jeff's character?

11. What did Jeff offer to Dicey?

12. Why was Sammy being rude to Jeff?

13. How is Jeff showing he has a crush on Dicey?

14. Why was the Thanksgiving meal special for the Tillerman's?

15. Who called to ask Sammy over to his house?

16. Why should the invite surprise the reader?

17. How does Mina see herself?

18. What does Mina think Sammy is fighting about?

19. How does Gram react to Dicey's statement about the reason why Sammy was fighting?

20. Who showed up while Dicey was working on the boat?

21. What did Maybeth do while Jeff played the guitar?

Chapter 9 Pages 267-297
1. What happened during recess at Sammy's school?

2. What did Gram call herself while at school?

3. How did the other kids react to Gram?

4. Why did Dicey ask Miss Eversleigh what she had said in class?

5. What did Dicey decide to do after speaking with Miss Eversleigh?

6. What news did Gram serve with the apple pie?

7. What was the first thing Gram said to Mina's father?

8. What did Jeff ask Dicey?

9. Why won't Dicey go with Jeff?

10. Why does Mina say Dicey isn't an easy person?

11. What does Dicey mean when she says, If you think about it, everybody has something wrong about them?"

12. Why were Gram and Dicey going to Boston?

13. What did Gram do to get the money for the airplane tickets?

14. Why did Mr. Lingerle act like Gram had paid him a compliment after telling him she knew he would look after the kids?

15. What did Mr. Lingerle give Gram before they boarded the plane?

16. What did Gram tell the nurse Dicey would be doing?

Essay Question: Explain how Gram's role in the kid's lives is changing with every day. Give specific examples of things Gram has done to demonstrate her role. How do you think Dicey is handling not having to be as responsible for her siblings as she once had been?

Chapter 10 Pages 298-324

1. What was wrong with Momma?

2. Why was the idea Dicey had in her mind of her Momma causing her such grief at the hospital?

3. Why did Dicey feel anger when she looked upon her mother?

4. Why did the doctor stress that Dicey's mother never *tried* to survive?

5. "Her fingers were numbed by the air, and she noticed a rim of dirty gray snow by the side of the road. Pieces of paper blew around on the sidewalk until they came to the edges of the buildings. There they nestled up forlornly." How does this quote convey the mood of the story?

6. Why did Dicey feel better after she bought the gloves for Gram?

7. What did Dicey buy for Sammy?

8. How does the shopping spree of Dicey's show another character trait of her?

9. What character trait would you give to Dicey?

10. Who had made the wooden chess set that Dicey wanted to get for James?

11. What did the color of the wooden bracelet remind Dicey of?

12. While in the wood shop, what did Dicey decide about Momma?

13. Why did Gram tell Dicey to let go?

Essay Question: How will the trip to Boston change Dicey forever?

_____
_____
_____
_____
_____
_____
_____
_____
_____
_____
_____
_____
_____
_____
_____
_____

Chapter 11 Pages 325-350

1. How much would it cost to send Momma home?

2. Where did Dicey take Gram to get an urn?

3. Why would the shop owner be honored if Gram took the box to be used as an urn?

4. How much money had Mr. Lingerle given Gram in the envelope?

5. What did James mean when he said that their mother had actually died last summer?

6. What do you think Gram meant when she told Dicey to let go, reach out, and hold on?

7. What did Dicey plan to do about John?

Essay Question: How has Mr. Lingerle proven himself as a friend to Gram?

_____
_____
_____
_____
_____
_____
_____
_____
_____
_____
_____
_____
_____

Chapter 12 Pages 351 – 359

1. Where did they bury Momma?
   _____

2. What did Gram bring down from the attic?
   _____

3. What had the Tillerman's never had that Mr. Lingerle was bringing for them?
   _____

4. Who looked like Bullet?
   _____

Essay Question: What do Gram's actions signify to the kids? How will her willingness to share change the family they have become?

_____
_____
_____
_____
_____
_____
_____
_____
_____

Character Trait Chart

Directions: Provide 3 examples of character traits for each character listed. Provide an example from the story to prove the trait you listed. Be sure to include a page number for each quote.

Character Name										
Dicey										
Gram										
James										

Dicey's Song A Novel Study

Internal/External Conflicts

Directions: Dicey and her family are dealing with many conflicts within the story. Complete the chart below to demonstrate your understanding of the conflicts taking place in the novel. Put your choice of a conflict occurring in the story in the last box.

Conflict	Explanation of Conflict
Dicey vs. herself	
Dicey vs. her teachers	
James vs. His intelligence	
Maybeth vs. Reading	
Dicey vs. Gram	

Cause and Effect Activity

Directions: Complete the cause and effect relationships listed below.

Cause	Effect

Essay Question: Explain how the cause/effect relationships move the story along.

_____
_____
_____
_____
_____
_____
_____
_____
_____

Analyzing the Title Activity

Directions: An author chooses the title of their novel for a specific reason. Evaluate the title of the novel and explain why it is or is not a good title.

1. **Does the title have a specific meaning to the book? If so, what is the meaning?**

   _____
   _____
   _____
   _____
   _____

2. **In the case of this novel, who or what does the title apply to?**

   _____
   _____

3. **Create a different title for the novel. Why do you think your title would/would not be a better title?**

   _____
   _____

4. **Comparing your title with the original, why is the original title better or worse than your choice?**

   _____
   _____
   _____
   _____
   _____
   _____

Analyzing Theme Activity

Directions: Discuss the theme or themes of the story.

Theme: A general idea or message normally concerned with life, human nature, or society the author is trying to relay to the reader. A theme is usually a universal idea (love vs. hate, loyalty vs. disloyalty, fairness) that is not stated directly by the author rather it is understood by the reader through the evidence provided in the storyline.

1. Brainstorm as many themes as you can for the story. Write them below.

   _____
   _____
   _____
   _____

2. Which theme idea do you feel is the most important to the story? Explain your answer.

   _____
   _____
   _____
   _____

3. Can there be more than one theme to a novel?

   _____
   _____

4. Of the themes you mention above, which one do you relate to the most and why?

   _____
   _____
   _____

Character Analysis Activity

Directions: The novel has provided extensive proof of each character's personality and traits. Choose a character you could identify with and explain why you felt a connection with that character. Be sure to include examples of the traits you claim they possess that drew you to them.

Plot Diagram

Directions: Starting at the beginning of the story, place the most important events in order on the plot diagram below.

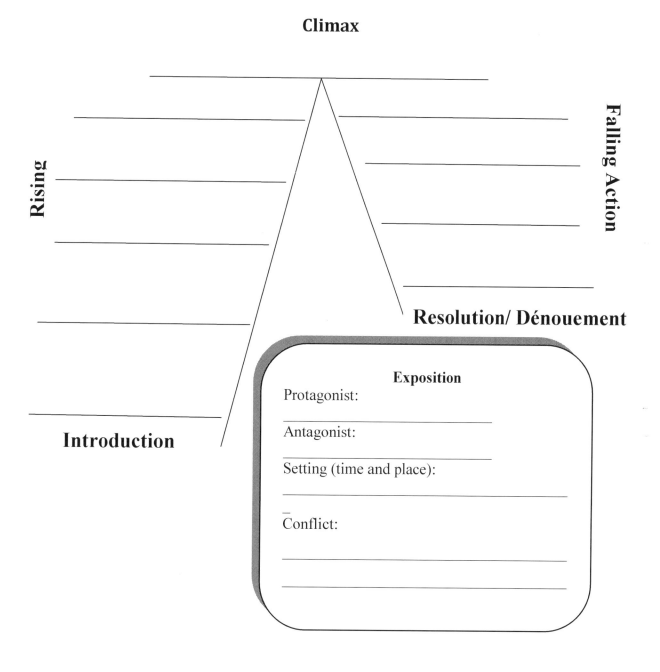

Dicey's Song A Novel Study

Plot Summary Essay

Directions: Using the Plot summary diagram, write an essay summarizing the plot of the story.

Teacher's Edition
(Answers NOT included for Graphic Organizers)

Vocabulary List Answers

1. chastened (52)
2. exhilarating (92)
3. envied (107)
4. sag (116)
5. appreciated (131)
6. extremes (138)
7. quivered (161)
8. curious (169)
9. eagerly (187)
10. exclusion (191)
11. impassive (200)
12. impatiently (205)
13. wisdom (218)
14. contentment (241)
15. emerged (248)
16. impressed (263)
17. charisma (280)
18. scurried (294)
19. reverberated (295)
20. solemn (327)

Directions: Put the words in alphabetical order on the lines below. Start from the beginning of the alphabet.

1. appreciated (131)
2. charisma (280)
3. chastened (52)
4. contentment (241)
5. curious (169)
6. eagerly (187)
7. emerged (248)
8. envied (107)
9. exclusion (191)
10. exhilarating (92)
11. extremes (138)
12. impassive (200)
13. impatiently (205)
14. impressed (263)
15. quivered (161)
16. reverberated (295)
17. sag (116)
18. scurried (294)
19. solemn (327)
20. wisdom (218)

Vocabulary Activity #1

appreciated	eagerly	extremes	reverberated
charisma	emerged	impassive	sag
chastened	envied	impatiently	scurried
contentment	exclusion	impressed	solemn
curious	exhilarating	quivered	wisdom

Directions: Unscramble the vocabulary word and write it on the space provided.

1. gas — sag
2. patimeitnyl — impatiently
3. dvneei — envied
4. dswmoi — wisdom
5. pmssaieiv — impassive
6. aaieeppcrtd — appreciated
7. degreme — emerged
8. eetttnocneenm — contentment
9. srcuuoi — curious
10. brrrvdteeeea — reverberated
11. eeemrtxs — extremes
12. caimasih — charisma
13. rrieudcs — scurried
14. dssrpmeei — impressed
15. eeaylgr — eagerly
16. lhixeeaigntr — exhilarating
17. mneols — solemn
18. drvuqiee — quivered
19. xlsncuioe — exclusion
20. denetsahc — chastened

© 2012 Jane Kotinek   Dicey's Song A Novel Study

Vocabulary Activity #2-Answers

appreciated	eagerly	extremes	reverberated
charisma	emerged	impassive	sag
chastened	envied	impatiently	scurried
contentment	exclusion	impressed	solemn
curious	exhilarating	quivered	wisdom

Directions: Find the missing vowels for each vocabulary word and write the vocabulary word on the space provided.

1. c__r__ __ __s   curious
2. r__v__rb__r__t__d   reverberated
3. __xtr__m__s   extremes
4. ch__r__sm__   charisma
5. sc__rr__ __d   scurried
6. __mpr__ss__d   impressed
7. s__g   sag
8. __mp__t__ __ntl__   impatiently
9. __nv__ __d   envied
10. w__sd__m   wisdom
11. __ppr__c__ __t__d   appreciated
12. __mp__ss__v__   impassive
13. c__nt__ntm__nt   contentment
14. __m__rg__d   emerged
15. ch__st__n__d   chastened
16. __xcl__s__ __n   exclusion
17. q__ __v__r__d   quivered
18. __xh__l__r__t__ng   exhilarating
19. s__l__mn   solemn
20. __ __g__rl__   eagerly

Vocabulary Activity #3

Directions: Use the dictionary guide words to decide whether the vocabulary word falls before the first guide word, between the guide words, or after the guide words. Place an X in the correct box.

Vocabulary Word	Guide Words	Before Guide Words	Between Guide Words	After Guide Words
appreciated	apothegm/applicator			X
charisma	chariot/ chaste		X	
chastened	charge/ chase			X
contentment	context/ continue	X		
curious	curate/curse		X	
eagerly	early/easel	X		
emerged	egg/eject			X
envied	entertain/envoy			X
exclusion	excoriate/exhale	X		
exhilarating	exhaust/exhort		X	
extremes	explosion/ extend			X
impassive	impair/imperious		X	
impatiently	impede/ import	X		
impressed	impost/improvise		X	
quivered	quintet/quoth		X	
reverberated	retch/return			X
sag	sage/saint	X		
scurried	scurvy/seal	X		
solemn	soda/solace			X
wisdom	wire/with		X	

Vocabulary Crossword Puzzle- Answers

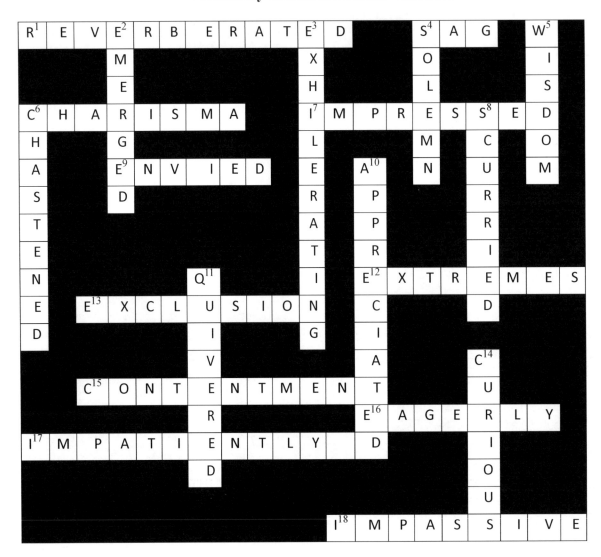

Across
1. To echo continuously
4. To droop, to lose firmness
6. A personal quality that produce feelings of devotion or enthusiasm
7. To affect favorably, to have left a mark
9. Felt resentment or jealously toward someone
12. Very intense, remote, to the greatest degree
13. Keep out, reject
15. The state of being satisfied, happy
16. Showing an interest in, enthusiastic about
17. Restlessly, anxiously
18. Expressionless, showing no emotion

Down
2. To come forth, to be revealed
3. Stimulating, energizing, elating
4. Gloomy, somber
5. Good judgment, knowing what is right
6. To reprimand or punish
8. To scamper or skitter about
10. To be aware of value or significance
11. To shake or vibrate
14. Questioning or prying

Dicey's Song A Novel Study

Chapter 1 pages 1-37
1. Where did Dicey and her family go to live? *They went to live with their Gram.*
2. What happened to Dicey's boat? *It had sunk.*
3. Why did Dicey want to fix the sailboat? *She considered it her lucky charm.*
4. What was the purpose of Dicey getting a job? *She wanted to bring money to the family.*
5. What is wrong with Maybeth? *She has difficulty learning in school.*
6. Why did Dicey go to Millie Tydings for a job? *She thought she could get a job there.*
7. What reasons did Dicey give for why Millie should hire her? *If the store were kept cleaner, people would shop there more often.*
8. How much money would Dicey earn per week at the grocery story? *She would earn $1.00 an hour.*
9. What did Gram say families always did first? *Took care of their own.*
10. Why does Gram have an appointment downtown? *To adopt the children.*
11. Where is Dicey's mom? *She is in a hospital.*
12. Why is Dicey's mother there? *She had a nervous breakdown.*
13. What did James point to in the Bible? *The names of his mother and uncles.*
14. What did Gram add to the Bible? *She wrote the names of the kids.*
15. Why does James wonder how things will be for them? *He wonders what will happen if it doesn't work out.*
16. How does Dicey show that she is maturing? *Answers will vary.*
17. What did Gram ask Dicey to help her with on Sunday? *She needed help with papers and pamphlets from the welfare department.*
18. What was on the table waiting for Dicey when she got home from school? *A letter.*
19. Who was the letter from? *It was from Maybeth's music teacher.*
20. Why was Dicey upset when she saw who had written the letter? *Maybeth had always done well in music class.*

Chapter 2 pages 38 – 66

1. What was the name of the girl in class who came up with interesting answers? *Wilhemina*
2. What was conflict was brought up in class by Wilhemina? *The conflict between an individual and the society he lives in.*
3. Who did Dicey see at the bike rack? *Jeff*
4. What was he doing? *He was playing the guitar.*

"Is it an hour already?" Millie asked. She turned over a fat wrist to look at her watch. "I'm being awful slow with this."

"You had interruptions," Dicey reminded her.

"That's right," Millie sounded surprised. She couldn't have forgotten, Dicey knew.

5. What, if anything, is the above quote foreshadowing? *Dicey recognizes that Millie needs her help.*
6. Why is Dicey upset that Sammy interrupted her while she was working on the boat? *She wanted to spend time by herself.*
7. Why wouldn't Dicey let Sammy help her? *He was too little and wouldn't do it correctly.*
8. Why did Mr. Lingerle want Maybeth to take special lessons? *She was musically talented.*
9. What was Dicey's idea to pay for Maybeth's lessons? *She would use the money from working for Millie.*
10. What did most of the people think about Gram? *They thought she was odd and outspoken.*
11. Who asked Dicey to be her science partner? *Wilhemina.*
12. What did Gram have for Dicey when she came home from school? *3 boys shirts.*
13. What did James hope to do for a job? *He wanted to get a newspaper route.*
14. What announcement did Sammy make in regards to helping James at his job? *He could ride his bike without getting tired.*
15. Why does Dicey feel as though everyone is turning away from her? *They were going to Gram more often with their problems.*

Chapter 3 Pages 67 – 102

1. What information did the letter concerning Dicey's mother contain? *There was no change in her mother.*
2. Why do you think Dicey keeps asking Gram what the letter says? *She is curious because it involves her mother.*
3. What was Dicey pleased about that Sammy wasn't doing at school? *He isn't fighting.*
4. What differences did Dicey see happening with
   Maybeth: *She was making friends.*
   Sammy: *He was not getting into trouble.*
   James: *He was working hard.*
5. What was the name of the person playing the guitar? *Jeff*
6. Why did Millie end up with so many boxes of corn flakes? *She ordered incorrectly.*
7. What solution did Dicey come up with to get rid of them? *They would have a sale.*
8. What reason did Millie give for not ordering correctly? *She never learned to read properly.*
9. What did Millie tell Dicey about the job at the grocery store? *She could keep it.*
10. Compared to her homework how did Maybeth perform on the piano? *She was exceptional on the piano.*
11. What did Gram make a dress out of for Maybeth? *An old shirt.*
12. What does this tell us about Gram's character? *She's resourceful.*
13. What did Cousin Eunice think of the Tillerman's? *She didn't want children.*
14. Why did she take the kids in? *She wanted others to think highly of her.*
15. Why did Mina accuse Dicey of being hard to befriend? *She was always on the defense.*

16. Who was the person at the piano waiting to speak to Gram? *Isaac Lingerle.*
17. Why did he have to wait to ask Gran a question? *Maybeth was working on her homework.*
18. While at dinner, what did Mr. Lingerle do that surprised Dicey? *He didn't eat as much as Dicey thought he would.*
19. What question did Mr. Lingerle ask Gram to convince her to let Maybeth have piano lessons? *He asked Gram if she wanted Maybeth to be successful.*
20. What was Mr. Lingerle going to charge for teaching Maybeth? *Nothing*
21. Why were the girls laughing at Dicey in Home EC class? *Her apron was funny looking.*

Essay Question: If Dicey were going to school with you, do you think you could be friends with her? Explain your answer.

Chapter 4 Pages 103 – 136

1. Why didn't Dicey want Sammy to bother her while she worked on the boat? *There was limited daylight.*
2. Why did Gram get upset with the kids for going up into the attic? *They had no business going into the attic.*
3. Why do you think Gram doesn't talk about her children? *There are too many painful memories.*
4. Who did Gram ask to watch the kids so she and Dicey could have a day out on Saturday? *Mr. Lingerle.*
5. Why didn't Gram like to be helped? *Answers will vary.*
6. Why did Dicey enjoy the shopping trip? *She liked watching people.*
7. What was Gram planning to do with the wool? *She was going to make sweaters.*
8. What is the progress of Maybeth's education? *She isn't improving.*
9. Why did Gram say Dicey deserved to enjoy their lunch at the restaurant without having to worry about the price? *They had problems to work on and needed the energy from the lunch.*
10. How long would Dicey have to worry about her brothers and sister? *For as long as she lived.*
11. Why did James write a different report? *He wanted to be accepted by his classmates.*
12. What does James like to work? *He likes working with his mind.*
13. Why did Gram want to get Dicey a jumper for school? *She had seen others wearing it. It was getting too cold for shorts.*
14. What did the saleslady say about Dicey? *She was beautiful.*
15. Why does Dicey want to ask James about Maybeth? *He is always good about coming up with ideas for solving problems.*

Chapter 5 Pages 136-169
1. Why did Dicey regret building a fire? *Mr. Lingerle wouldn't leave.*
2. Why did Gram tell Mr. Lingerle he might as well stay while they discussed Maybeth? *He knew her too.*
3. Why was Gram disappointed with James' ideas about Maybeth? *She thought he could do better.*
4. What does James think is the problem with Maybeth? *She's not making the connection between what she sees and what her brain tells her.*
5. What is his suggestion for Maybeth? *Maybeth should work on reading the letters rather than the whole word.*
6. Why did Dicey feel the hopelessness surrounding Maybeth fading away? *She realized they actually had a plan that might work.*
7. What is Gram teaching Maybeth to do? *She is teaching her to knit.*
8. What kind of relationship, outside of brother/sister, do Dicey and Sammy appear to have? *They have a mother/son relationship.*
9. Why does Sammy get upset with Dicey when he visits her by the boat? *She ignores him.*
10. Why was Sammy excited when Dicey asked him to get the sandpaper? *He wanted to help.*
11. Why doesn't Sammy play games during recess at school? *He doesn't want to get angry and explode.*
12. Why does Sammy think it's his fault about his mother leaving? *He should have behaved better.*
13. What was Sammy trying to convince Gram to buy? *Chickens.*
14. Whose house would James visit for the first time? *Toby's.*
15. Explain why this was considered a big deal for him? *He didn't usually have friends.*
16. Why hasn't James come up with a solution for Maybeth? *He's been putting it off.*
17. Why was Maybeth upset when she returned from school? *All the kids had laughed at her when she tried to read aloud.*
18. What did James tell Maybeth he was going to do for her? *He was going to teach her to read.*
19. What did James want to use to teach Maybeth? *Phonics*
20. What was his reasoning for his decision? *It was used for a long time and it was how he had learned to read.*

Chapter 6 Pages 170-192
1. What grade did Dicey receive in Home Ec? *She received an F.*
2. Why was Dicey upset about the grade? *She had done all of the assignments.*
3. Why was Dicey confused about the grade she received in English? *She had only earned A's and B's.*

4. Why did Dicey feel like hugging Gram after they had discussed her report card? *Gram believed what Dicey had told her about the grades.*
5. Who came into Millie's store while Dicey was working? *Jeff*
6. What did Millie say Gram was like in school? *She had been a handful.*
7. Why did Dicey need to wait for Sammy? *He had been in detention.*
8. Why did Sammy kiss Margaret? *He had lost a bet trying to do pull-ups.*
9. What did Maybeth tell Dicey about learning to read? *She thinks the new way of learning is working.*
10. Why did Dicey have an easy time planning a budget with $50? *She had done it before when her mom had left them.*
11. What did Miss Eversleigh do to Dicey's paper with the meals on it? *She had given it an F.*
12. Why didn't Dicey care what Miss Eversleigh thought or said? *What more could Miss Eversleigh do? She had already flunked Dicey.*

Essay Question: Why do you think Dicey shows little concern about the grades she receives in Home Ec? What does this tell us about her character?

Chapter 7 Pages 193- 22

1. Explain Dicey's thoughts on grades and the importance of assignments. *Everything a teacher had to say they gave in the grade.*
2. What had happened to Dicey's mom? *She had a nervous breakdown.*
3. What compliment did Mina give to Dicey? *She said Dicey would never cheat.*
4. What was Mr. Chappelle accusing Dicey of doing with her story? *He was accusing her of plagiarism.*
5. How did Dicey react to Mr. Chappelle's accusation? *She didn't say a word.*
6. What did Mina say about Dicey to defend her to Mr. Chappelle? *She doesn't care enough about what others think to cheat on something.*
7. How did Mina prove Dicey had written the essay? *She asked her if she were related to the person in the essay.*
8. What did Mr. Chappelle do when Dicey picked up her essay? *He gave her an A+ and apologized.*
9. Why do you think Gram forced Dicey to discuss the English paper? *Answers will vary.*
10. What did Gram tell Dicey after she had read Dicey's essay? *She said it was good.*
11. What did Gram say about her marriage to John? *It was not a good marriage.*
12. What did Gram say the purpose of the essay was? *The essay was a kind of reaching out on Dicey's part.*
13. Why did Mina's dad reprimand Dicey when she called? *It was too late to be calling.*
14. Why did Dicey call Mina? *She wanted to say "thank you" to her.*

15. Why would Gram worry about what Mina's parents think about her? *Her father was a preacher.*

Chapter 8 Pages 223-266
1. Why didn't Millie ask Dicey for her work paper? *She probably didn't know she should.*
2. Why do you think Dicey didn't mind Mina asking if the essay were about Dicey's momma? *She felt a connection with Mina.*
3. Why was Sammy at the grocery store when Dicey got there? *He couldn't ride the bus for a week.*
4. Why won't Sammy tell Dicey about the fight he was involved in? *Answers will vary.*
5. Why did James act like he didn't care who Sammy had fought? *He hoped Sammy would tell him.*
6. Why doesn't Maybeth like Ernie? *He's a bully.*
7. What bargain did Gram try to make with Sammy in connection with the marbles? *She'd play if he told her what happened.*
8. Describe Sammy. *(Page 233)*
9. How does Dicey see Jeff? *(Page 235)*
10. How would you describe Jeff's character? *He is friendly, considerate, and compassionate.*
11. What did Jeff offer to Dicey? *He offered her a ride home.*
12. Why was Sammy being rude to Jeff? *He was probably jealous.*
13. How is Jeff showing he has a crush on Dicey? *Answers will vary.*
14. Why was the Thanksgiving meal special for the Tillerman's? *They had never celebrated it before this year.*
15. Who called to ask Sammy over to his house? *Ernie*
16. Why should the invite surprise the reader? *He was the bully.*
17. How does Mina see herself? *(page 250)*
18. What does Mina think Sammy is fighting about? *She thinks he is fighting about Gram.*
19. How does Gram react to Dicey's statement about the reason why Sammy was fighting? *She got very quiet.*
20. Who showed up while Dicey was working on the boat? *Jeff*
21. What did Maybeth do while Jeff played the guitar? *She sang while he played.*

Chapter 9 Pages 267-297
1. What happened during recess at Sammy's school? *Gram went to his school and played marbles. She won all of the marbles.*
2. What did Gram call herself while at school? *The Lone Marble Ranger.*
3. How did the other kids react to Gram? *They thought she was great. Maybe a little crazy.*
4. Why did Dicey ask Miss Eversleigh what she had said in class? *She hadn't been listening.*

5. What did Dicey decide to do after speaking with Miss Eversleigh? *She would try to acquire the skills taught by Miss Eversleigh.*
6. What news did Gram serve with the apple pie? *The kids were legally, officially, and permanently, Gram's responsibility.*
7. What was the first thing Gram said to Mina's father? *"I've come to put a face on the bogeyman."*
8. What did Jeff ask Dicey? *He asked her if she would go to a dance with him.*
9. Why won't Dicey go with Jeff? *She was only in the 8th grade.*
10. Why does Mina say Dicey isn't an easy person? *Answers will var.*
11. What does Dicey mean when she says, If you think about it, everybody has something wrong about them?" *Answers will vary.*
12. Why were Gram and Dicey going to Boston? *They were going to visit Dicey's mother.*
13. What did Gram do to get the money for the airplane tickets? *She sold the cranberry spoon.*
14. Why did Mr. Lingerle act like Gram had paid him a compliment after telling him she knew he would look after the kids? *He wanted to please Gram.*
15. What did Mr. Lingerle give Gram before they boarded the plane? *He gave her an envelope with money in it.*
16. What did Gram tell the nurse Dicey would be doing? *She would be going up to her mother's room.*

Chapter 10 Pages 298-324
1. What was wrong with Momma? *She was in a coma. She was dying.*
2. Why was the idea Dicey had in her mind of her Momma causing her such grief at the hospital?
3. Why did Dicey feel anger when she looked upon her mother? *She felt her mother had given up.*
4. Why did the doctor stress that Dicey's mother never *tried* to survive? *She wouldn't eat.*
5. "Her fingers were numbed by the air, and she noticed a rim of dirty gray snow by the side of the road. Pieces of paper blew around on the sidewalk until they came to the edges of the buildings. There they nestled up forlornly." How does this quote convey the mood of the story? *It seems like there is no hope. The mood is very sad and depressing.*
6. Why did Dicey feel better after she bought the gloves for Gram? *She was happy she had bought Gram something she needed.*
7. What did Dicey buy for Sammy? *A toy airplane.*
8. How does the shopping spree of Dicey's show another character trait of her? *She is very practical and thoughtful.*
9. What character trait would you give to Dicey? *Answers will vary.*
10. Who had made the wooden chess set that Dicey wanted to get for James? *The shop owner.*

11. What did the color of the wooden bracelet remind Dicey of? *Her mother's hair.*
12. While in the wood shop, what did Dicey decide about Momma? *Answers will vary.*
13. Why did Gram tell Dicey to let go? *Answers will vary.*

Chapter 11 Pages 325-350
1. How much would it cost to send Momma home? *$700.*
2. Where did Dicey take Gram to get an urn? *She took her to the store with the wood chess set.*
3. Why would the shop owner be honored if Gram took the box to be used as an urn? *He knew Dicey appreciated his craftsmanship and he wanted her to have something nice for her mother.*
4. How much money had Mr. Lingerle given Gram in the envelope? *$500.*
5. What did James mean when he said that their mother had actually died last summer? *She had given up hope when she abandoned them.*
6. What do you think Gram meant when she told Dicey to let go, reach out, and hold on? *Answers will vary.*
7. What did Dicey plan to do about John? *She would contact him.*

Chapter 12 Pages 351 – 359
1. Where did they bury Momma? *They buried her beneath the paper mulberry tree.*
2. What did Gram bring down from the attic? *Photo albums.*
3. What had the Tillerman's never had that Mr. Lingerle was bringing for them? *He was getting them pizza.*
4. Who looked like Bullet? *James looks like Bullet.*

Assessments
With Answers

Dicey's Song
Quiz 1 Chapters 1 – 3

Directions: Choose the best answer for each question.

1. Why was Dicey fixing the sailboat?
   A. She wanted a means to escape.
   B. It was her lucky charm.
   C. She wanted to give it to James as a present.
   D. She wanted to surprise Gram with it.

2. Why did Dicey want to get a job?
   A. She needed supplies for the boat.
   B. She wanted to buy new clothes.
   C. She wanted to bring money into the household.
   D. She knew the kids would need things for school.

3. What reason did Dicey give Millie for hiring her?
   A. She was a hard worker.
   B. She had a lot of friends who would come to the store.
   C. She needed the money.
   D. She would clean the store so more people would shop there.

4. What did Gram intend to do with the children?
   A. She was going to send them to their aunt.
   B. She was going to adopt them.
   C. She was going to send them to an orphanage.
   D. She didn't know what she was going to do with them.

5. Why was Dicey upset about the note sent home from school by Maybeth's teacher?
   A. Maybeth was good in music.
   B. It was too early in the school year for notes.
   C. She didn't want any problems for Gram.
   D. She didn't want to hear bad news.

6. Why won't Dicey let Sammy help her on the sailboat?
   A. She wants time by herself.
   B. She thinks he will ruin the sailboat.
   C. He will talk the whole time he is in there.
   D. He will only anger Dicey.

Dicey's Song
Quiz 1 Chapters 1 – 3

7. What type of job did James get?
   A. He would deliver groceries.
   B. He was going to mow lawns.
   C. He would deliver the newspaper.
   D. He would help around in the library.

8. What did the letter tell Dicey about her mother?
   A. She would be leaving the hospital around Thanksgiving.
   B. She was improving.
   C. She was eating better.
   D. She was not improving.

9. Why did Millie end up with extra boxes of corn flakes?
   A. She wanted to have a sale with them.
   B. They were listed very cheaply.
   C. She never learned to read properly.
   D. She thought she would need them for the holiday coming up.

10. What word best describes Gram?
    A. Resourceful
    B. Out-going
    C. Overly friendly
    D. Ignorant

11. Why did Cousin Eunice take the kids in?
    A. She felt sorry for them.
    B. She always wanted kids.
    C. She wanted to look good for her friends.
    D. She always adored Dicey.

12. Who wants to give Maybeth piano lessons?
    A. Millie
    B. Mr. Lingerle
    C. Mina
    D. Mr. Chappelle

Dicey's Song
Quiz 1 Chapters 1 – 3

13. Why were the girls laughing at Dicey during home ec class?
    A. Her apron was funny looking.
    B. She had just told a joke.
    C. Her cake had burned in the oven.
    D. She didn't know how to turn the sewing machine on.

14. How are the kids changing?
    A. They are doing stuff for themselves.
    B. They are becoming angrier every day.
    C. They are forgetting about their mother.
    D. They are relying on Gram more than Dicey.

15. The mood of the story is-
    A. adventurous.
    B. solemn.
    C. contented.
    D. mysterious.

Dicey's Song
Quiz 2 Chapters 4 – 6

Directions: Choose the best answer for each question.

1. Where did Gram take Dicey on their Saturday together?
   A. The library.
   B. The attorney's office.
   C. The mall.
   D. To visit her mother.

2. What was the other reason for the Saturday excursion?
   A. To discuss the problems the kids were having.
   B. To figure out a game plan for the adoption.
   C. To check out flights to Boston.
   D. To buy cows for Sammy.

3. How long would Dicey have to worry about her brothers and sister?
   A. Just until they graduated.
   B. Until Gram could get on her feet financially.
   C. As long as she was alive.
   D. Until her mother came home.

4. How is James different from Sammy?
   A. James likes to work with his mind.
   B. James is a fighter.
   C. Sammy is a gifted thinker.
   D. James gets into trouble a lot.

5. Why was Gram disappointed with the suggestion given by James to help Maybeth?
   A. She thought he could have done better.
   B. She wasn't impressed because she could have come up with the idea.
   C. She thought he would have had several ideas.
   D. She felt he didn't put his best effort forward for his favorite sister.

6. Why doesn't Sammy play games during recess?
   A. He doesn't like playing games.
   B. He needs to study during recess.
   C. He doesn't want to get angry.
   D. He hates recess.

Dicey's Song
Quiz 2 Chapters 4-6

7. What is Sammy trying to do convince his Gram to buy for him?
    A. Cows.
    B. A dog.
    C. A kitten.
    D. Chickens

8. Why did James want to use phonics to teach Maybeth to read?
    A. Phonics was for stupid kids.
    B. He didn't think she could handle anything else.
    C. He learned to read using phonics.
    D. He didn't know how to teach reading any other way.

9. Why was Dicey upset about the grade she received in home ec?
    A. She had done her best.
    B. She had done all of the assignments.
    C. She had produced good assignments.
    D. She had finished most of her assignments.

10. Why did Sammy have to serve detention?
    A. He got into a fight.
    B. He disrespected a teacher.
    C. He said a bad word.
    D. He kissed a girl.

Dicey's Song
Quiz 3 Chapters 7 – 8

Directions: Choose the best answer for each question.

1. What had happened to Dicey's mom?
    A. She died in a freak accident.
    B. She ran away with her fiancé.
    C. She had a nervous breakdown.
    D. She went to Europe.

2. What compliment did Mina give to Dicey?
    A. Mina said Dicey would never cheat.
    B. Mina said Dicey looked pretty.
    C. She said she liked Dicey's new jumper.
    D. She said she wished she were as smart as Dicey.

3. What did Mr. Chappelle accuse Dicey of doing?
    A. Writing Mina's essay.
    B. Not submitting an essay.
    C. Cheating on her essay.
    D. Letting Mina write her essay.

4. How did Mina know Dicey was innocent?
    A. Mina had written her own essay.
    B. Dicey would never let anyone write an essay for her.
    C. Dicey didn't care what others thought about her.
    D. She had watched Dicey write her essay.

5. What did Gram say was the purpose of the essay?
    A. The purpose was for Dicey to learn how to write better.
    B. It was a way to express her thoughts in a clear, concise way.
    C. It was a way for Dicey to be noticed.
    D. It was a way for Dicey to reach out.

6. Why was Sammy at the grocery store when Dicey got there.
    A. He had been kicked off the bus.
    B. He would be working at the store with Dicey.
    C. He was waiting for Gram to pick him up.
    D. He was going to help James.

Dicey's Song
Quiz 3 Chapters 7 – 8

7. What word best fits Jeff?
   A. A nuisance.
   B. Compassionate
   C. A showoff
   D. Rude

8. Why was the Thanksgiving meal special for the kids?
   A. They loved turkey.
   B. It meant Christmas was right around the corner.
   C. They didn't have to go to school.
   D. It was the first time they had celebrated it.

9. What did Mina say Sammy was fighting about?
   A. He was feeling neglected by Dicey?
   B. He didn't feel as though he were included in the family.
   C. Kids were picking on him.
   D. Something had been said about Gram.

10. How is the relationship between Dicey and Mina developing?
    A. They are in competition with one another.
    B. They have a mutual respect for each other.
    C. They cannot tolerate each other.
    D. They feel they have to stick together to survive.

Dicey's Song
Quiz 4 Chapters 9-12

Directions: Choose the best answer for each question.

1. Why did Gram go to the school?
   A. She needed to have a conference with Sammy's teacher.
   B. To talk to the principal.
   C. To play marbles with Sammy and his friends.
   D. To change him out of math class.

2. What news did Gram give the kids while they ate apple pie?
   A. They would be moving.
   B. Their mother would be home soon.
   C. She was going to Boston.
   D. She had legally adopted them.

3. What question did Jeff ask Dicey that she said no to?
   A. He asked her to sing with him.
   B. He asked her to be his girlfriend.
   C. If she would like a ride home.
   D. If she would go to the dance with him.

4. Why did Dicey and Gram go to Boston?
   A. They went shopping.
   B. They needed to see the attorney.
   C. They went to see Dicey's mother.
   D. They had never been on a plane before.

5. Who would be watching the kids while they were gone?
   A. Mr. Chappelle.
   B. Mr. Lingerle
   C. Millie
   D. James

6. What did Mr. Lingerle give to Gram before she boarded the plane?
   A. He hugged her.
   B. He kissed her.
   C. He gave her a letter.
   D. He gave her an envelope.

Dicey's Song
Quiz 4 Chapters 9-12

7. How did Gram get the money for the plane tickets?
   - A. She sold the cranberry spoon.
   - B. She used the welfare money.
   - C. She used the money from Mr. Lingerle.
   - D. She sold the sailboat.

8. What did the colors in the bracelet remind Dicey of?
   - A. A rainbow.
   - B. The shimmer on the lake.
   - C. Her mother's hair.
   - D. The sun shining through the kitchen window.

9. What will Dicey do about her uncle John?
   - A. She will write him a letter asking him to take the kids.
   - B. She will contact him.
   - C. She will do nothing because Gram wouldn't like her to talk to him.
   - D. She will call him when Gram is out of town.

10. What did Gram bring down from the attic?
    - A. A Christmas tree.
    - B. Photo albums.
    - C. Winter clothes.
    - D. Toys

Dicey's Song
Comprehension Test

Directions: Choose the best answer for each question.

1. Why was Dicey fixing the sailboat?
    A. She wanted a means to escape.
    B. It was her lucky charm.
    C. She wanted to give it to James as a present.
    D. She wanted to surprise Gram with it.

2. Why did Dicey want to get a job?
    A. She needed supplies for the boat.
    B. She wanted to buy new clothes.
    C. She wanted to bring money into the household.
    D. She knew the kids would need things for school.

3. What reason did Dicey give Millie for hiring her?
    A. She was a hard worker.
    B. She had a lot of friends who would come to the store.
    C. She needed the money.
    D. She would clean the store so more people would shop there.

4. What did Gram intend to do with the children?
    A. She was going to send them to their aunt.
    B. She was going to adopt them.
    C. She was going to send them to an orphanage.
    D. She didn't know what she was going to do with them.

5. Why was Dicey upset about the note sent home from school by Maybeth's teacher?
    A. Maybeth was good in music.
    B. It was too early in the school year for notes.
    C. She didn't want any problems for Gram.
    D. She didn't want to hear bad news.

6. Why won't Dicey let Sammy help her on the sailboat?
    A. She wants time by herself.
    B. She doesn't think he will do a good job.
    C. He will talk the whole time he is in there.
    D. He will only anger Dicey.

Dicey's Song
Comprehension Test

7. What type of job did James get?
   A. He would deliver groceries.
   B. He was going to mow lawns.
   C. He would deliver the newspaper.
   D. He would help around in the library.

8. What did the letter tell Dicey about her mother?
   A. She would be leaving the hospital around Thanksgiving.
   B. She was improving.
   C. She was eating better.
   D. She was not improving.

9. Why did Millie end up with extra boxes of corn flakes?
   A. She wanted to have a sale with them.
   B. They were listed very cheaply.
   C. She never learned to read properly.
   D. She thought she would need them for the holiday coming up.

10. What word best describes Gram?
    A. Resourceful
    B. Out-going
    C. Overly friendly
    D. Ignorant

11. Why did Cousin Eunice take the kids in?
    A. She felt sorry for them.
    B. She always wanted kids.
    C. She wanted to look good for her friends.
    D. She always adored Dicey.

12. Who wants to give Maybeth piano lessons?
    A. Millie
    B. Mr. Lingerle
    C. Mina
    D. Mr. Chappelle

Dicey's Song
Comprehension Test

13. Why were the girls laughing at Dicey during home ec class?
    A. Her apron was funny looking.
    B. She had just told a joke.
    C. Her cake had burned in the oven.
    D. She didn't know how to turn the sewing machine on.

14. How are the kids changing?
    A. They are doing stuff for themselves.
    B. They are becoming angrier every day.
    C. They are forgetting about their mother.
    D. They are relying on Gram more than Dicey.

15. The mood of the story is-
    A. Adventurous
    B. Solemn
    C. Thoughtful
    D. Mysterious

16. Where did Gram take Dicey on their Saturday together?
    A. The library.
    B. The attorney's office.
    C. The mall.
    D. To visit her mother.

17. What was the other reason for the Saturday excursion?
    A. To discuss the problems the kids were having.
    B. To figure out a game plan for the adoption.
    C. To check out flights to Boston.
    D. To buy cows for Sammy.

18. How long would Dicey have to worry about her brothers and sister?
    A. Just until they graduated.
    B. Until Gram could get on her feet financially.
    C. As long as she was alive.
    D. Until her mother came home.

Dicey's Song
Comprehension Test

19. How is James different from Sammy?
    A. James likes to work with his mind.
    B. James is a fighter.
    C. Sammy is a gifted thinker.
    D. James gets into trouble a lot.

20. Why was Gram disappointed with the suggestion given by James to help Maybeth?
    A. She thought he could have done better.
    B. She wasn't impressed because she could have come up with the idea.
    C. She thought he would have had several ideas.
    D. She felt he didn't put his best effort forward for his favorite sister.

21. Why doesn't Sammy play games during recess?
    A. He doesn't like playing games.
    B. He needs to study during recess.
    C. He doesn't want to get angry.
    D. He hates recess.

22. What is Sammy trying to do convince his Gram to buy for him?
    A. Cows.
    B. A dog.
    C. A kitten.
    D. Chickens

23. Why did James want to use phonics to teach Maybeth to read?
    A. Phonics was for stupid kids.
    B. He didn't think she could handle anything else.
    C. He learned to read using phonics.
    D. He didn't know how to teach reading any other way.

24. Why was Dicey upset about the grade she received in home ec?
    A. She had done her best.
    B. She had done all of the assignments.
    C. She had produced good assignments.
    D. She had finished most of her assignments.

Dicey's Song
Comprehension Test

25. Why did Sammy have to serve detention?
    A. He got into a fight.
    B. He disrespected a teacher.
    C. He said a bad word.
    D. He kissed a girl.

26. What had happened to Dicey's mom?
    A. She died in a freak accident.
    B. She ran away with her fiancé.
    C. She had a nervous breakdown.
    D. She went to Europe.

27. What compliment did Mina give to Dicey?
    A. Mina said Dicey would never cheat.
    B. Mina said Dicey looked pretty.
    C. She said she liked Dicey's new jumper.
    D. She said she wished she were as smart as Dicey.

28. What did Mr. Chappelle accuse Dicey of doing?
    A. Writing Mina's essay.
    B. Not submitting an essay.
    C. Cheating on her essay.
    D. Letting Mina write her essay.

29. How did Mina know Dicey was innocent?
    A. Mina had written her own essay.
    B. Dicey would never let anyone write an essay for her.
    C. Dicey didn't care what others thought about her.
    D. She had watched Dicey write her essay.

30. What did Gram say was the purpose of the essay?
    A. The purpose was for Dicey to learn how to write better.
    B. It was a way to express her thoughts in a clear, concise way.
    C. It was a way for Dicey to be noticed.
    D. It was a way for Dicey to reach out.

Dicey's Song
Comprehension Test

31. Why was Sammy at the grocery store when Dicey got there.
    A. He had been kicked off the bus.
    B. He would be working at the store with Dicey.
    C. He was waiting for Gram to pick him up.
    D. He was going to help James.

32. What word best fits Jeff?
    A. A nuisance.
    B. Compassionate
    C. A showoff
    D. Rude

33. Why was the Thanksgiving meal special for the kids?
    A. They loved turkey.
    B. It meant Christmas was right around the corner.
    C. They didn't have to go to school.
    D. It was the first time they had celebrated it.

34. What did Mina say Sammy was fighting about?
    A. He was feeling neglected by Dicey?
    B. He didn't feel as though he were included in the family.
    C. Kids were picking on him.
    D. Something had been said about Gram.

35. How is the relationship between Dicey and Mina developing?
    A. They are in competition with one another.
    B. They have a mutual respect for each other.
    C. They cannot tolerate each other.
    D. They feel they have to stick together to survive.

36. Why did Gram go to the school?
    A. She needed to have a conference with Sammy's teacher.
    B. To talk to the principal.
    C. To play marbles with Sammy and his friends.
    D. To change him out of math class.

Dicey's Song
Comprehension Test

37. What news did Gram give the kids while they ate apple pie?
    A. They would be moving.
    B. Their mother would be home soon.
    C. She was going to Boston.
    D. She had legally adopted them.

38. What question did Jeff ask Dicey that she said no to?
    A. He asked her to sing with him.
    B. He asked her to be his girlfriend.
    C. If she would like a ride home.
    D. If she would go to the dance with him.

39. Why did Dicey and Gram go to Boston?
    A. They went shopping.
    B. They needed to see the attorney.
    C. They went to see Dicey's mother.
    D. They had never been on a plane before.

40. Who would be watching the kids while they were gone?
    A. Mr. Chappelle.
    B. Mr. Lingerle
    C. Millie
    D. James

41. What did Mr. Lingerle give to Gram before she boarded the plane?
    A. He hugged her.
    B. He kissed her.
    C. He gave her a letter.
    D. He gave her an envelope.

42. How did Gram get the money for the plane tickets?
    A. She sold the cranberry spoon.
    B. She used the welfare money.
    C. She used the money from Mr. Lingerle.
    D. She sold the sailboat.

Dicey's Song
Comprehension Test

43. What did the colors in the bracelet remind Dicey of?
    A. A rainbow.
    B. The shimmer on the lake.
    C. Her mother's hair.
    D. The sun shining through the kitchen window.

44. What will Dicey do about her uncle John?
    A. She will write him a letter asking him to take the kids.
    B. She will contact him.
    C. She will do nothing because Gram wouldn't like her to talk to him.
    D. She will call him when Gram is out of town.

45. What did Gram bring down from the attic?
    A. A Christmas tree.
    B. Photo albums.
    C. Winter clothes.
    D. Toys

Assessment Answers

Quiz 1
1. B
2. C
3. D
4. B
5. A
6. A
7. C
8. D
9. C
10. A
11. C
12. B
13. A
14. D
15. C

Quiz 2
1. C
2. A
3. C
4. A
5. A
6. C
7. D
8. C
9. B
10. D

Quiz 3
1. C
2. A
3. C
4. C
5. D
6. A
7. B
8. D
9. D
10. B

Quiz 4
1. C
2. D
3. D
4. C
5. B
6. D
7. A
8. C
9. B
10. B

Comprehension Test
1. B
2. C
3. D
4. B
5. A
6. A
7. C
8. D
9. C
10. A
11. C
12. B
13. A
14. D
15. C
16. C
17. A
18. C
19. A
20. A
21. C
22. D
23. C
24. B
25. D
26. C
27. A
28. C
29. C
30. D
31. A
32. B
33. D
34. D
35. B
36. C
37. D
38. D
39. C
40. B
41. D
42. A
43. C
44. B
45. B

Thank you for purchasing this novel study. Please consider my other novel studies available for sale.

Novel Studies by Jane Kotinek:

Among the Hidden A Novel Study

Fever, 1793 A Novel Study

Gregor the Overlander A Novel Study

Guardians of Ga'Hoole: The Capture A Novel Study

Guardians of Ga'Hoole: The Journdey A Novel Study

Island Book One: Survival A Novel Study

Island Book Three: Escape A Novel Study

Island Book Two: Survival A Novel Study

Island Trilogy Three Novel Studies

Nory Ryan's Song A Novel Study

Pendragon: The Merchant of Death A Novel Study

Pictures of Hollis Woods A Novel Study

Princess Academy A Novel Study

Ranger's Apprentice: The Ruins of Gorlan A Novel Study

Rules A Novel Study

The Boy Who Dared A Novel Study

The Clay Marble A Novel Study

The Looking Glass War A Novel Study

The Tale of Depereaux A Novel Study

Made in the USA
Columbia, SC
08 September 2022